"Like Ungaretti and Apollinaire, Julien Vocance faced the instant karma of the First World War with outcries of visionary perception. Each flash of the battlefield, each haiku, is a compelling ode to what can go away in a second, and to what remains, even amid annihilation. *One Hundred Visions of War* is an essential addition to the history of modernist poetry. More importantly, it is an urgent and deeply moving read, each vision guided into English by the poet Alfred Nicol, who brings a keen eye, an exacting ear, and a consummate poetic intelligence to these pages."

—Joseph Donahue, Professor of the Practice at Duke University; author of the ongoing poem *Terra Lucida*

"Don't miss reading Julien Vocance's *One Hundred Visions of War*, marvelously translated by Alfred Nicol. Drawing from the brevity of traditional Japanese haiku, Vocance's fascinating French *haï-kaï* bear witness to the horrors of war in bursts of image and sensation. The trenches of WWI materialize on the page by way of language both fresh and timeless."

—Kirun Kapur, Editor of *Beloit Poetry Journal*; author of *Women in the Waiting Room*

"When I learned that the French poet Julien Vocance chose to write his *One Hundred Visions of War* in—of all things!—hai-ku, I wondered why: how could that most fleeting, elusive, and subtle of forms deal with a theme as dense, brutal, and unsubtle as the horror that is war? Well, I've just read—and reread, nonstop—Alfred Nicol's brilliant translation of the French original, and the only thing I'm wondering now is how I managed to undervalue so completely what imagination, speed, daring imagery, black humor and an uncanny gift for language can do to convey the unspeakable perfectly."

—Rhina P. Espaillat, 2021 Recipient of the NEPC Golden Rose Award; author of *And After All*

"Holy shit."

—Joshua Mehigan, Author of *Accepting the Disaster*, a *New York Times Book Review* best book of the year

ONE HUNDRED
VISIONS OF WAR

Translated from the French by Alfred Nicol

Julien Vocance

Printed in the United States of America

Set in Baskerville Typesetting

Cover Design: Amanda Brown

Interior image from Katshushika Hokusai's series of woodblock prints, "One Hundred Views of Mt. Fuji."

Paperback ISBN-13: 978-1-951319-37-3

Poetry / French Poetry

CONTENTS

PREFACE

Dana Gioia

No nation suffered worse casualties or physical destruction in the Great War than France, which was the scene of the largest and most sustained fighting. The French army eventually called up nearly nine million men to defend the six thousand miles of trenches that divided the Allies from the German army. Early losses were so substantial that men up to forty-five were conscripted. The French army eventually suffered six million casualties, including 1.4 million dead. Almost three-quarters of those who fought were killed, wounded, or lost in action.

The Battle of Verdun left 700,000 casualties, not counting the "lightly wounded." Losses were nearly equal on each side. There were too many corpses to be adequately counted or buried. Verdun was only one battle. In 1914 alone France and the Allies engaged in some of the largest military engagements in human history at Marne, Ypres, and Champagne.

Post-war France was a nation full of the blind, the crippled, the scarred, and the shell-shocked. America's "lost generation" consisted of spiritually confused emigrees living in Paris. The lost generation of France lay in cemeteries, hospitals, and sanitaria. They shuffled as amputees on village streets or hid their disfigured faces behind painted copper masks.

How did the human imagination comprehend the nature and extent of the carnage? Old worldviews no longer fit the horrific reality. Artists had to reimagine the modern world and develop ways to present it truthfully. The result was the transformation of the nascent Modernist movement into the dominant form of artistic expression across Europe and the Americas. Since the Modernist impulse had originated in France, it found immediate and multifarious forms there. American readers generally have a limited sense of the vast literature that emerged from the conflict. Most of the major French works spawned by the war remain unknown in English. It may be illuminating to summarize a few.

The visionary poet Charles Péguy, who died in the Battle of the Marne, saw the massacre as redemptive national sacrifice consecrating the soil of France.

Blessed are those who died in great battles.
Stretched out on the ground in the face of God.
Blessed are those who died on a final high place,
Amid all the pomp of grandiose funerals.

Blessed are those who died for carnal cities.
For they are the body of the city of God.
Blessed are those who died for their hearth and fire,
And the lowly honors of their father's house.

Péguy's approach served the needs of public ceremony in Catholic France—sonorous sentiments to comfort survivors. Had he lived to see the final outcome of the war, I think he would have regretted those lines. Being beautiful did not make them true. Sacramental violence offers no redemptive grace.

The more common literary response was that of Louis-Ferdinand Céline, who was wounded in the Battle of

Flanders leaving his right arm partially paralyzed. For him, the horror of mechanized mass murder destroyed the moral authority of society. The experience left him bereft of moral vision to guide his cynical satiric genius. Despite his fascist allegiances and anti-Semitism, Céline's nihilistic anger remained influential into the Existentialist period, and one still sees his shadow today in Michel Houellebecq.

Guillaume Apollinaire, who coined the term *surrealism*, thrilled at the violent spectacle of battle. "Soldiering is my true profession," he boasted. "I so love art," he told a friend, "that I have joined the artillery." He never fully recovered from a shrapnel wound that tore open his head in 1915. He died from influenza at 38 a few days before the Armistice. His truest response to the war was *Les mamelles de Tirésias, The Breasts of Tiresias* (1918), a surreal farce in which a woman becomes a man and invents a baby-making process that produces 40,049 children in a single day. Drafted before the war, Apollinaire revised his "*drame surréaliste*" to reflect the realities of 1917. Its absurd ingenuity was a hilarious evasion of the national nightmare—amusing to the degree one forgets why France needed all those new bodies. "Listen closely to the lessons of war," the play concludes gleefully, "and make babies as never before!"

Péguy, Céline, and Apollinaire are brilliant writers, but their works suggest the impossibility of any comprehensive artistic response to the European apocalypse. Each author offered a dazzling tableau colored by his own tortured experience. In those tragic years, French history had become psychohistory. It helps to consider these estimable writers to assess the imaginative and moral power of another less celebrated work, Julien Vocance's *Cent visions de guerre, One Hundred Visions of War*, first published in 1916.

Joseph Seguin, who published under the name Julien Vocance, provides a more cogent response to the holocaust of the Western Front. The poet, who lost an eye in the trenches of Champagne, crafted one of the clearest and objective records of the conflict. He avoided the hypnotic spell of traditional meters—the glorious traditional music of Péguy. He also rejected the avant-garde glorification of violence—with its priapic cannons and flowering explosions—that Lieutenant Apollinaire absorbed from Futurism. Vocance sought clarity not enchantment. He found a moral stance without any taint of moralism by adopting a radical new form into French, the Japanese haiku, or as he called it *haikai—les epigrammes lyrique du Japon*." The effect was a Modernist mixture of the realist and lyric modes.

To reach my skin, how
would bullets ever get through
my crusted woolens?

. . .

Bombs, bombs and more bombs—
but we don't take up much space:
our chances are good.

The choice of haiku as the form of Vocance's long poem was revolutionary. The haiku had only just entered Western poetry. Yone Noguchi's "A Proposal to American Poets" (1904) brought the "hokku" into English and inspired Ezra Pound's fascination with the form. The French introduction to the haiku began at the same time through the translations and poems of Paul-Louis Couchoud in *Au fil de l'eau, Along the Waterway* (1905). The haiku was still viewed mostly as a short lyric form. In neither language had such an ambitious Modernist sequence been attempted.

Vocance's extraordinary *One Hundred Visions of War* has a simple but ambitious design. It presents a soldier's experience of the Western Front in one hundred discrete imagistic moments. There is no narrative framework, except the implied passing of time. Each section is self-contained. One can read the individual haiku as separate lyric poems, but the sections gain a collective resonance as the sequence proceeds. Vocance allows the reader to see the battlefield at ground level in one sudden moment of clarity after another. Most of these "visions" are small, but some are panoramic. The compression and sensuous quality of the haiku communicate the moments in experiential terms. (The work's title and numeration make bitter allusion to Katsushika Hokusai's exquisite collection of woodblocks, *One Hundred Views of Mt. Fuji*.) Vocance's poems are both visual and visionary but never grandiose. He reports rather than philosophizes. Only at the end does he venture a well-earned conclusion:

Two rows of trenches,
Two lines of barb-wire fences:
Civilization.

One Hundred Visions of War is a major poetic testament of the Great War. Few works of such audacious originality are so accessible and emotionally engaging. More than a century after its publication, Vocance's sequence has lost neither its shock value nor its strange tenderness. Alfred Nicol deserves every accolade for his brilliant and affecting translations. He has restored a lost masterpiece to English-language memory.

INTRODUCTION

Alfred Nicol

The "One Hundred Visions of War" of Julien Vocance (1878-1954) comprise some of the first haiku written in the West. Vocance's *haï-kaï,* as he called them, break nearly all of the rules of classical Japanese haiku, because of the situation he found himself in when mobilized into the French infantry in 1914. Where classical haiku traditionally speaks of the beauty of Nature, the change of seasons, and, occasionally, domestic events, Vocance uses the form to depict the horror and brutality of armed conflict, as seen from the trenches during the first world war. Readers get a ground-level view of unimaginable slaughter. The value of his poetry lies not in its adherence to classical rules of composition, but in its witness to the experience of the human being caught up in a battle which, as Wendell Berry put it, "the machines won."

The tension between the traditional subjects and themes of haiku and the use Vocance makes of it serves to heighten the expressive power of Vocance's *Visions.* For that reason, I have chosen to count syllables in making these translations, adhering to the traditional 5-7-5 pattern, as Vocance himself did not, to ensure that these short poems are recognizable to contemporary readers as the haiku he clearly intended them to be—the title of this work itself makes reference to Katshushika Hokusai's famous series of woodblock prints, "One Hundred Views of Mt. Fuji."

Vocance was thirty-six years old when the war began. Like so many of the trench soldiers he wrote about, he lost an eye in battle, but he managed to survive the brutal experience, and was awarded the *Croix de Guerre* for his service.

Julien Vocance was the pen name taken by Joseph Sequin, who returned to his position in the Ministry of Public Works after the war. This work first appeared in *La Grande Revue* in 1916, under the title "Cent visions de guerre." Vocance later published two collections, *Le Livre des haï-kaï,* which included "One Hundred Visions of War," and *Le Héron Huppé.*

*   *   *

Miller, Paul, "Essay on the Haiku of Julien Vocance (Part I) by Paul Miller; Haiku Translated by Paul Miller and Petra Jenkins.," *The Haiku Foundation Digital Library*, accessed August 25, 2022 https://www.thehaikufoundation.org/omeka/items/show/6212.

Vocance, J., 2017. *Cien visiones de guerra.* Translated by S. Benet. Sevilla, Spain: Renacimiento.

ONE HUNDRED

VISIONS OF WAR

Written in 1916, in the mud of the trenches

Blackening three months
between the trenches, the dead
have lost all their hair.

Rumors of widows
and orphans swarm over
these poor pale bodies.

Death, no doubt, dug
and watered these deep furrows
where men are planted.

Just pulled my head in,
there's a mosquito whine and
the ridge collapses.

At ground level
fifteen days, I recognize
every clump and weed.

In dirt-colored clothes,
men in furrows shovel dirt.
There's glory for you.

Night comes, once so sweet,
now ripped with sudden flashes.
Shadows dance, fiercely.

Two men in a hole
in the ground, at night, facing
a massive army.

A ball of fire
vanishes into a cloud:
Moses on Sinai.

We get a quick look
around when bursts of gunfire
light the horizon.

Fireworks fill the sky.
Yet another sacrilege
over these mass graves.

When the searchlight falls
on the trench-diggers, they fling
themselves to the ground.

Crushed by exhaustion,
they take the collapsed postures
of fallen corpses.

Out of the east springs
the dragon, spitting red teeth.
Pull the canvas shut.

At dawn,
greedily, they gulp
cold soup.

Shrieking as it climbed,
but taking its own sweet time,
the shell passed us by.

A brown swirl
of shells rolling in the dirt
like schoolboys.

The small, gray-breasted
taube[*] dropping its pigeon shit:
a bomb or rocket.

* *The taube was an early German monoplane. In German, the word literally means dove.*

A llama, spitting
mad: the 77*
firing from the mill

* *The 7.7 FK 96, a field gun used by Germany in World War I.*

The cannons tonight
shake with such violent coughing
it can't last. It can't.

Shells come crashing in
shy of our trenches—breakers
that don't reach the shore.

"Shells coming toward us!
Hurry! Hurry! We'll get buried!"
Rookie reaction.

In clotted dribbles,
fanning out around the man,
his flesh spurted out.

Every day, you see
new ones spring up from the ground:
white wooden crosses.

A movement of troops;
the noise of cracked tambourines
fading in the fog.

Crouched in our dugouts,
where the cyclone of iron
may leave us alone.

Four plumes of black smoke
and the whole earth shakes.
Where next?

The flesh convulses
sensing the hurtling grapeshot
about to enter.

Scalding hiss, cat squall,
screech, grind, whirring . . . And all that
banging of scrap iron!

To be made aware
that all existence ends in
hunger, cold, and fear

The shell left a hole.
Reflected in its water,
heaven. All of it.

Iron gray, lead gray,
ash gray, resignation gray . . .
Let's spruce this place up!

Vampires: the shells
tear up cemetery slabs,
toppling their crosses.

Charred, my cathedral,
you'll be still more beautiful,
no less eternal.

Castles from legends,
market towns from old etchings,
all razed in one day.

Little girl, you've lost
an arm. That's no way to play.
You could be my Vieve.

Grumbling in a shack,
the woman worked hard all year.
"Where did it get me?"

Trench soldier
A genuine man of the woods
Gorilla

To reach my skin, how
would bullets ever get through
my crusted woolens?

Into his flannels
go his fingernails, pecking
at the little beasts.

He saw his name there.

He read the schoolgirl's letter.

"What the fuck is this?"

Ruddy complexion,
belly unbuttoned:
officers' cook.

They pat their bellies,
polish them like chalices.
March? They could never.

In the vertebrae
of a horse buried in haste
my foot made a mush.

A wriggling beetle,
upside down on the slick slope,
pinned by his pack's weight.

If you see smoke trails,
follow them to find the plane . . .
But not in the sky.

A sea of fire!
The shells set the swamp ablaze.
The vines are crackling.

Soft footsteps
here in this desolate place . . .
My eyes frisk the dark.

The advance lookout
trips on a gangrenous corpse,
beats a quick retreat.

Fetal position:
if my head's not cold my feet
stick out and freeze—

Stop panting like that.
Yeah, yeah, you're covered in blood—
A bullet grazed you.

Yesterday, whistling
in my ears. Today, my cap.
Tomorrow, my head.

The stain keeps growing;
he's turning into one of
Garibaldi's redshirts.

Lark, that song of yours
is obscene! But no, it's just
Nature's indifference.

Smelly old field mice,
at least you don't sing. We share
one bowl, one shelter.

Tonight, we head toward
the cannons. Alas, poor flesh,
that awful voice calls.

The cannons exhale
flames, like blasts from a forge—
panting from slaughtering.

Terror in his eyes,
his own death snarling at him,
he bolts from the trench.

Cla cla cla cla cla . . .
—like a skeleton counting
fingers on its teeth.

Bloody machine gun.
Before it died, it spread out
its fan of corpses.

Bombs, bombs and more bombs—
but we don't take up much space:
our chances are good.

The young men's bodies
celebrate bloody weddings,
clinging to the earth.

Tunnels the mines dig
extend into the forest.
Cracks in the pines blaze.

Skimming the trenches,
the Minenwerfer,* screeching
like an angry cat

Minenwerfer ("mine launcher" or "mine thrower") is the German name for a class of short range mine shell launching mortars used extensively during the First World War by the Imperial German Army. The weapons were intended to be used by engineers to clear obstacles, including bunkers and barbed wire, that longer range artillery would not be able to target accurately.

To their frugal meal
a black sausage is added,
smashing three chests.

We'll bury you, sure.
Only so your rotting flesh
doesn't poison us.

In his dimming eyes
the paralyzing memory:
his wife, his children—

Beneath the wrinkles
of fallen, washed-out khakis,
piles of ash gather.

Nights, we carry to
the white wooden burial place
victims of the day.

Strapped in the canvas
a comrade shoulders—slaughtered meat
a mother waits for

Far off,
dogs howling at death . . .
They're getting closer . . .

Poison snakes
thrown into the night, hidden
somewhere in the vines

Black birds in wild flight
gaining speed, coming this way,
shells swoop down.

Five yellow mummies
bathe in the reddened water
of the trenches, bombed.

A beautiful glow! . . .
Put your hands on your eyelids
to protect yourself.

Blood spilled, washed with rain,
muddied, dried . . . Bright crimson blood,
so colorless now.

You'll later regret
this missed opportunity—
to die in your sleep.

Scrap-metal-pierced skin
Eardrums beaten thin
Home with no way in

Fraying gauze
Faded clothes
Faces closed

White linen, white walls,
white tiles . . . Our sickly pallor
works like camouflage.

Men full of shrapnel
tied to their beds and collared—
like they might run off!

Faces gashed and scarred;
pitiful, loathsome bodies
no woman will love.

Wise, those on stretchers
wait their turn before entering
the cage of wild beasts.

Warm, like her eyes, soft
like her voice, her hands can heal,
she thinks. I believe.

Freed from this bloodbath,
beneath the evening lamp, safe,
holding you near me . . .

All swaddled in white,
dressed for the sarcophagus:
no hands, feet, or face.

With our bandaged heads,
we look like we're going to
give praise to Allah.

Get it in the eye
you're a hero. Not me, though—
got it in the ass.

Savage warriors!
Just show them a child's booboo
and they fall apart.

Memories haunt him
tonight. The thermometer
reads 40°*.

* (104° F)

Near the feverish man
with nightmares, the cardplayers
deal another hand.

The young nun is thrilled
to have that sketch of Jesus
the soldier gave her.

Young girls came around
with candy "suckers" for us.
Big hit, those "suckers."

Having comforted
the maimed, the consul's wife left.
Now, maybe, we'll eat.

Their eyes are shining
with health, youthfulness, and hope.
Bright eyes—made of glass.

This is the realm where
shadows feel their way along
through an endless night.

He's left the battle,
the old vet. The post-war years
will tear him to shreds.

He stopped and sat down,
obstructing an entrance way,
his chin on his knees.

Comrades, my brothers,
we've suffered a lot . . . Enough.
Go win without me.

Two rows of trenches,
Two lines of barbed-wire fences:
Civilization.

Acknowledgments

Thanks to the editors of *The Lowell Review*, *The Hypertexts*, and *Beltway Poetry Quarterly*, where sections of this work in translation first appeared.

Thanks, too, to Rhina Espaillat, first reader of my manuscript, and to Midge Goldberg for her valuable critique.

ABOUT THE TRANSLATOR

Alfred Nicol worked in the printing industry for twenty years after graduating from Dartmouth College, where he received the Academy of American Poets Prize. He now lives in West Newbury, Massachusetts. A longtime member of the Powow River Poets, he edited the *Powow River Anthology*, published by Ocean Publishing in 2006. Nicol was the recipient of the 2004 Richard Wilbur Award for his first book of poems, *Winter Light*, published by The University of Evansville Press. His other publications include *Animal Psalms* (Able Muse, 2016); *Elegy for Everyone* (Prospero's World Press, 2009); and *Brief Accident of Light: Poems of Newburyport*, a collaboration with Rhina P. Espaillat (Kelsay Books, 2019). His poems have appeared in *Poetry, The New England Review, Dark Horse, Commonweal, The Formalist, The Hopkins Review*, and *The Best American Poetry 2018*.

Visit his website at alfrednicol.com.